RAÚL ZURITA (b. 1950) was born in Santiago de Chile. In 1973 he was arrested by the Pinochet regime and imprisoned in the hold of a ship. He was a founder of the group Colectivo Acciones de Arte (CADA), which undertook extremely risky public-art actions against the regime. In 1982 five airplanes wrote his poem "La Vida Nueva" in the sky above New York City, and in 1993 he had the phrase "NEITHER PAIN NOR FEAR" bulldozed into the Atacama Desert in a permanent, two-mile-long installation, visible only from above. Zurita received the Chilean National Prize for Literature in 2000 and the Asan Memorial World Poetry Prize in 2018.

WILLIAM ROWE's *Collected Poems* were published in 2016 by Crater Press. He has translated a number of Latin American poets, including Rodolfo Hinostroza, Juan L. Ortiz, Hugo Gola, Magdalena Chocano, Néstor Perlongher, and Mario Montalbetti. *Three Lyric Poets*, his study of Lee Harwood, Chris Torrance, and Barry MacSweeney, was published in 2009.

NORMA COLE is a poet, painter, and translator. Her most recent books of poetry include *Fate News*, *Actualities*, *Where Shadows Will*, and *Win These Posters and Other Unrelated Prizes Inside*. Her translations from French include Danielle Collobert's *It Then*, the anthology *Crosscut Universe: Writing on Writing from France*, and Jean Daive's *White Decimal*. Cole lives and works in San Francisco.

T0286658

Raúl Zurita

INRI

TRANSLATED FROM THE SPANISH
BY WILLIAM ROWE
PREFACE BY NORMA COLE

NYRB/POETS

nyrb   NEW YORK REVIEW BOOKS   *New York*

THIS IS A NEW YORK REVIEW BOOK
PUBLISHED BY THE NEW YORK REVIEW OF BOOKS
435 Hudson Street, New York, NY 10014
www.nyrb.com

Library of Congress Cataloging-in-Publication Data
Names: Zurita, Raúl author. | Rowe, William, translator. | Cole, Norma,
  author of introduction.
Title: Inri / by Raúl Zurita ; translated by William Rowe ; introduction by
  Norma Cole.
Other titles: Inri. English
Description: New York : New York Review Books, 2018. | Series: New York
  Review Books poets
Identifiers: LCCN 2018024724| ISBN 9781681372785 (alk. paper) | ISBN
  9781681372792 (epub)
Classification: LCC PQ8098.36.U75 I5713 2018 | DDC 861/.64—dc23
LC record available at https://lccn.loc.gov/2018024724

ISBN 978-1-68137-278-5
Available as an electronic book; ISBN 978-1-68137-279-2

Cover and book design by Emily Singer

Printed in the United States of America on acid-free paper.
10 9 8 7 6 5 4 3 2 1

For Paulina Wendt who gave this book its title
and me a heaven I no longer hoped for

Contents

SEA OF PAIN is an invitation from Raúl Zurita. In 2016 at the Kochi-Muziris Biennale in Kerala, India, in a dilapidated colonial warehouse, Zurita created an installation of seawater and poetry, and dedicated it to Galip Kurdi, the brother of Aylan Kurdi. Fleeing Syria, both children drowned in the Mediterranean on September 2, 2015, and Galip's body was never found. The iconic photograph of Aylan, whose body washed up on the sand near Bodrum, Turkey, as though in a "children's graveyard," was taken by the Turkish photographer Nilüfer Demir. "There are no photographs of Galip Kurdi, he can't hear, he can't see, he can't feel. He is a representative of the other faceless forgotten in other crises and conflicts around the world," the poet says. "I am not his father, but Galip Kurdi is my son." As you walk through knee-deep seawater, you read the poem written on canvases on the walls:

In the Sea of Pain

Don't you listen?

Don't you look?

Don't you hear me?

Don't you see me?

Don't you feel me?

In the sea of pain

Won't you come back, never
again, in the sea of pain?

"If water has memory, it will also remember this," says Raúl Zurita in *The Pearl Button*, a film by Patricio Guzmán. About this installation, Zurita says, "It's hope for the world, which has no hope. Possibility for the world that has no possibility. It's love for the world that has no love." It's the experience of love that infuses *INRI*.

Experience, from the Latin *experire*, means to undergo, endure, suffer. To feel, from the Latin noun *periculum*, which means danger, risk. What is at stake here? On the morning of September 11, 1973, the armed forces of Chile staged a coup. While the Palacio de La Moneda was being attacked, President Salvador Allende died and soon after General Augusto Pinochet established a military dictatorship. In Valparaíso, where he had been an engineering student, Zurita and thousands of others were rounded up and herded into the National Stadium. Zurita, along with around eight hundred others, were then packed into the hold of a ship and tortured. Some, like Zurita, were eventually let go. During those years, thousands of people "disappeared." The authorities would not tell what had happened to them.

Zurita chose to stay in Chile, enduring the brutal seventeen-year dictatorship when he could have gone into exile like so many others who feared for their lives. There is power and agency in staying in a dangerous place when one has the choice to leave. "I had to learn how to speak again from total wreckage, almost from madness, so that I could still say something to someone," Zurita writes in a note about *INRI*, at once making clear the immediate context for its composition.

On January 8, 2001, in a nationally televised speech, social-democratic President Ricardo Lagos announced, with brevity, information pertaining to those who were still un-accounted for in the government-sponsored killings during the 1970s. These missing people had been kidnapped by the security forces and tortured, their eyes gouged out, and their bodies thrown from helicopters "into the ocean, the lakes, and the rivers of Chile." And the Atacama Desert in the north. People knew about it, but there was no corroboration. Then suddenly there was.

Looking for the disappeared was "a thorn in the country's soul." After this announcement, Viviana Díaz, the president of the Association of Families of the Detained and Disappeared, said, "I've spent my whole life looking for my father. Now I know I'll never find him.... To discover that he is in the depths of the ocean is terrible and distressing." Even though, as Zurita says, they knew what had happened, the actual acknowledgment, the validation, came as a shock and a rupture in time. Reports and evidence of committed poured forth. Not needing to prove the facts anymore, what does the tragedy mean? How do you carry on? How do you hold the remembering, the identification, the trauma that took place, is still taking place, taking space "to represent a memory"?

As Emmanuel Lévinas wrote in *Existence and Existents*, "Being remains, like a field of forces." From the horror that was and still is, Zurita embraces the disappeared, loving and naming them again and again, "stopping the wounds with his fingers," touching and giving us raised dots of braille letters with the particularity of fingertips, "accustomed always to follow yours."

In *On Collective Memory*, Maurice Halbwachs observes, "While the collective memory endures and draws strength from its base in a coherent body of people, it is individuals as group members who remember." Loose or raw memory requires a frame. Zurita says, in an interview with Daniel Borzutzky, one of his translators, "Forgetting is impossible. But what you do with that memory, what you do with that inability to forget is a different story. I think that, in terms of this reality, you are obligated to a certain intensity, a certain force.... Even if it's completely utopian, completely mad, the force to continue [means] wagering on the possibility of the construction of a paradise," and he cites Ezra Pound, Canto CXX:

I have tried to write Paradise

Do not move

Let the wind speak
that is paradise.

Robert Duncan writes, "Poetry was a communal voice
for us—it spoke as we could not speak for ourselves." From
1979 to 1986, a collective was created called CADA (Colec-
tivo Acciones de Arte), which included Zurita, Fernando
Balcells, Diamela Eltit, Lotty Rosenfeld, and Juan Castillo.
Under the military dictatorship this was dangerous, but it
was the choice at the time. Using materials at hand—spray
paint, flyers, trucks, public space, and direct action, with
the body as the medium of expression for the creation of a
social and political art, everyone performed. This form be-
came part of the creative process. "NO + (NO más=NO
more)" was adopted as the slogan, first in Santiago, then all
over the country. On June 2, 1982, in New York City, CADA
used the sky as a page. Five airplanes composed fifteen lines
of Zurita's "La Vida Nueva" in the cloudless blue.

In the preface to *Purgatory* in 1979, translated by Anna
Deeny, Zurita imagines "these poems occupying land-
scapes." In 1993, he has a line from "La Vida Nueva" bull-
dozed into the Atacama Desert: "NI PENA NI MIEDO"
("NEITHER PAIN NOR FEAR"). Because of the scale—two
miles in length—the tracks can't be read as writing unless
seen from above, from the sky. Could this be an atavistic
remembering of the largest prehistoric anthropomorphic
figure in the world, the Atacama Giant, the geoglyph of
Cerro Unita? At 390 feet in length, it is the calendar for the
setting of the moon, used to conjecture the rains, to plant
crops. Zurita says, "My attempt has been to pull poetry and

nature together, because in the end they are the same. I have always been startled by work that refuses to acknowledge the limits of human capacity."

At the end of his 745-page tome *Zurita* (2011), he includes photographs from a future project involving an intervention in the physical landscape called "Your Life Breaking." The photographs of the sea cliffs in northern Chile have phrases typed out across them to show the compelling installation Zurita has envisioned. These phrases, corresponding to the table of contents of *Zurita*, include: "You Will See Soldiers at Dawn," "You Will See the Snows of the End," "You Will See Cities of Water," "You Will See What Goes," "You Will See Not Seeing," and "And You Will Weep." You will see them from the ocean.

Since the 1970s, critics have been writing about the "expanded field" and the blurring of the boundaries between land art and poetry, but this doesn't really apply here because there is no boundary. Zurita's installations and performative works are transdisciplinary. These poetic works are at the same time in process and timeless, boundless and intimate. Earth, sky, and water are incomparable sheets to be written upon, discovered, recovered.

"Without poetry, it's possible that violence would be the norm, the steady state, but because poems exist, all violence is unjustifiable, is monstrous," Zurita has said. Francine Masiello has written in *The Art of Transition* that the "ethics of representation" are a "splintering of any totalizing vision" and "stands as a form of rebellion against state patterns of fixed representation...the expression of choice is...in the fragment." The fragment evokes the sublime, how it startles itself and others. If beauty is about harmony, the sublime is disharmony, fragmentation, disruption, being on the brink, the edge of the cliff, looking out onto the numinous inconceivable. The sublime can be characterized as representing pain and pleasure in the infinite, the unknown, the limitless, beyond comprehension, beyond measure, unbounded, unthinkable, untenable, unutterable.

In *Purgatory*, Zurita silently screams, "EL INRI ES MI MENTE EL DESIERTO DE CHILE" ("THE INRI IS MY MIND THE DESERT OF CHILE"). With his immersive approach, he can already say that the INRI doesn't "come into mind" because, like the desert, it's already in mind, in his mind. Human=Nature. As Spinoza says in *Ethics*, "Each thing tends to persevere in its being. The individual therefore tends toward its limit."

In an interview with Ilan Stavans, Zurita says that when he was very young his Italian grandmother read him passages, parts of stories, from the *Inferno*. She also told him about her home in Rapallo, and about many Italian artists. Perhaps she showed him images, such as Michelangelo's Sistine Chapel, his *Creation of Adam*, Adam, the figure of humanity, his finger almost touching God's. What does it mean that Dante's *Commedia* was told to him, like spells, in his formative years by his grandmother?

For Zurita there are many iterations of *Paradiso*. He's been working on the question of Paradise at least since the coup. From the preface of *Anteparadise*, translated by Jack Schmitt, "we should keep on proposing Paradise, even if the evidence at hand might indicate that such a pursuit is folly."

Then, "I'll never write a Paradise, even if such a thing were to be written today." And from *¿Qué es el Paraíso?* (1979) —"fragment encountered among the ruins"—Zurita sets out to be "a worker of Paradise, not only of art but of experience." He proposes Paradise as a "project of the construction of a new feeling and a new social form of experience" that can transform "pain into the collective construction of new meaning."

INRI is a volume constructed of love and shame and mortification. The disappeared were innocents and they belong in Paradise. Through the gospels, the prophets, and Dante, the poet screaming is not holding his hands to his ears to block that screech. Rather, he is permitting the screech to blow, to explode, to translate it into a loving, startling requiem, with the Latin title for Jesus of Nazareth, King of the Jews: Iesvs Nazarenvs Rex Ivdaeorvm. And as the epigraph tells us, "if they keep silent, the stones will cry out" (Luke 19:40). Pain, "the black hole of language," becomes elegy, the formal lament for the dead, the turbulence creating palpable love, resurrection. Writing his *Paraíso* through the *Paradiso*, the poet shows us how he is working his way from bitterness and outrage, from rain and sea to the desert, from light to sight, from horror to love, "Love! By whom Heaven is ruled" (Dante, *Paradiso*, translated by Reverend Henry Cary, published in 1850). From *INRI*, in William Rowe's astonishing translation, the ostinato of names and loves flow forth—"unfinished loves," "hundreds of loves," "love cut short," "goodbyes cut short," "my love letters," and "a new love." The stretto, the breaking in, increases the emotional tension. The rain of baits becomes the rain of grace. Light brings sight, broken bodies become whole, reuniting with their souls. And "when ye shall again regain your visible forms, / the sight may without harm endure the change" (Dante, *Paradiso*).

"From centre to the circle, and so back, / From circle to the centre, water moves / In the round chalice, even as the blow / Impels it" (Dante, *Paradiso*). Similarly, in Zurita's fugue, the water moving, waves of water moving are understood as a discourse, the lines of the poem moving. And yet the water, like verse, is finite in volume. The verses of *INRI* cycle from moving to unmoving, temporality giving way to the atemporal, "and they were the plains once more." Waves read as currents in the sky, patterns in the desert and in one's ear. Murmuring a hymn, they crescendo into the ecstatic, in language, to narrate the passion, the blow—the coup. We, like the poet, remember the multitude of innocents. The "Epilogue": "They are dead." We call their names.

—*Norma Cole*

INRI

Author's Note

IN JANUARY 2001, on TV, the President of Chile, Sr. Ricardo Lagos, acknowledged that the bodies of hundreds and hundreds of people who had been disappeared during the Pinochet dictatorship would never be found because they had been thrown out of airplanes into the sea and the mountains: into the Pacific Ocean and into the mouths of volcanoes. The message was brief and it was something all of us had known for many years. I had myself published in Chile in 1985 during the dictatorship a book called *Canto a su amor desaparecido* (*Song for His Disappeared Love*), which took those crimes as its main theme. A line from that book is inscribed on the Memorial to the Disappeared in Santiago.

As I say, it is not something that should have surprised me, at least not any more than the horrors experienced every day (I had always stayed in Chile) for so many years. But there was still something about the acknowledgment, perhaps the formality of the act beside the magnitude of what was being acknowledged, or possibly the ridiculous pretense of solemnity in the face of sheer brutality, that made me feel ashamed in a way that nothing that had happened to me as an individual had made me feel ashamed. No, it wasn't "moral outrage" or any other high-sounding phrase, it was something much more concrete and unspoken: it was like a screech I couldn't get away from, that I may never be able to pull myself away from. The book was called *INRI*, and it came out of the image of a man who was uttering strange words on the TV. I don't know if what I am saying about the screech makes sense: It was called innrrrrrrriiiiiiiiiiiiiiiiiii.

There was also a detail, another fact about that crucifixion. One of the reports tells how before killing their victims the military personnel gouged out their eyes with hooks. That is why in the book no one sees, they only hear. It's that. I finished this book a year after the image I had remembered at the beginning; and I think I understood that the only final respect and acknowledgment for thousands and thousands of human beings has been the acknowledgment and respect of the land.

Yes, dear sea, beloved volcanoes, deserts, and glaciers. They have been the poems, not shame like a screech, not the stench of truth uttered too late.

Raúl Zurita
Santiago, May 2005

*For all the rose-pink tombs
of the sea, rivers, and cordilleras* of Chile*

---

* The mountain chain of the Andes, whose peaks, the highest in South America, can be seen rising above the narrow coastal plain of Chile.—*Trans.*

I

And I say to you, if they keep silent, the stones will cry out.

— LUKE 19:40

The Sea

Strange baits rain from the sky. Surprising bait falls upon the sea. Down below the ocean, up above unusual clouds on a clear day. Surprising baits rain on the sea. There was a love raining, there was a clear day that's raining now on the sea.

They are shadows, bait for fishes. A clear day is raining, a love that was never said. Love, ah yes, love, amazing baits are raining from the sky on the shadow of fishes in the sea.

Clear days fall. Some strange baits with clear days stuck to them, with loves that were never said.

The sea, it says the sea. It says baits that rain and clear days stuck to them, it says unfinished loves, clear and unfinished days that rain for the fish in the sea.

You can hear whole days sinking, strange sunny
mornings, unfinished loves, goodbyes cut short
that sink into the sea. You can hear surprising
baits that rain with sunny days stuck to them,
loves cut short, goodbyes that not anymore.
Baits are told of, that rain for the fish in the sea.

The blue brilliant sea. You can hear shoals of fish
devouring baits stuck with words that not, days
and news that not, loves that not anymore.

It is told of shoals of fish that leap, of whole
whirlwinds of fish that leap.

You can hear the sky. It is told that amazing
baits rain down with pieces of sky stuck to them
upon the sea.

I heard a sea and a sky hallucinated, I heard suns exploding with love fall like fruits, I heard whirlwinds of fish devouring the pink flesh of surprising baits.

I heard millions of fish which are tombs with pieces of sky inside, with hundreds of words that were never said, with hundreds of flowers of red flesh and pieces of sky in the eyes. I heard hundreds of loves that were stopped on a sunny day. Baits rained from the sky.

Viviana cries. Viviana heard whirlwinds of fishes rise up in the air fighting for mouthfuls of a goodbye cut short, of a prayer not heard, of a love not said. Viviana is on the beach. Viviana today is Chile.

The long fish that is Chile rises up through the air devouring the baits of sun that are its dead.

Tremendous plains rain down for the fishes:
days that will now never be, eyes stuck to a final
sky, loves that were not said. It says tremendous
plains made of arms that couldn't embrace, of
hands that didn't touch. It says strange fruits
that the fish devour, that the silver tombs which
are the fish devour. I heard extraordinary plains
raining on the sea.

Extraordinary skies, days, dreams sinking into
the silver whirlpools of waves, I heard the silver
mouths of fish devouring unfinished goodbyes. I
heard immense plains of love saying that no
more. Angels, musical scores of love saying no
more.

Universes, cosmoses, unfinished winds raining
down in thousands of pink baits on the
carnivorous sea of Chile. I heard plains of love
never said, infinite skies of love sinking into
the carnivorous tombs of the fish.

Here is the sea, it says, the carnivorous tombs of the fish. Here is the almond-colored flesh and the sea. The sea weeps. Viviana weeps.

There are infinite skies of almond trees, of stars, like fruits, they say, and fall. Surprising baits fall from the sky like the stars, like fruits that fall on the grass. There are endless universes in the fishes' stomachs, stars, almond orchards. Viviana hears immense orchards of blood-red almond trees falling onto the sea. Infinite clear days raining on the red foam of the sea.

People rain down and fall in strange positions like rare fruit of a strange harvest.

Viviana hears surprising human baits raining down, amazing human fruit harvested in strange fields. Viviana is now Chile. She hears human fruit raining down like golden suns exploding on the waters.

Amazing harvests rained out of the sky.
Incredible ripe fruit upon the ploughed fields of
the sea. Viviana hears mute silhouettes fall,
minutes that did not finish, sacred crosses that
rain like clouds upon the waves of the Pacific.
She hears torsos, strange mists coming off the
waves, strange clouds of soft flesh against the
empty sky of the ocean.

Baits rain down with mouthless angels, with
scores that could not be heard, with soundless
shadows that kiss. Amazing harvests rain down.
crash down, extraordinary trees that fall
burning into the waves.

Ploughed fields, sacred lands rain from the sky
with broken backs, pieces of necks that weren't
there anymore, unexpected clouds of unending
spring. They were thrown. They rain down.
Amazing harvests of people come down as food
for the fish in the sea. Viviana hears sacred lands
rain down, hears her son fall like a cloud onto
the unclouded cross of the Pacific.

Crosses made of fish for the Christs. The arch of the Chilean sky falls on the bloody tombs of Christ for the fishes. That's your mother, there. That's your son. Shadows fall on the sea. Strange human baits fall on the crosses of fish in the sea. Viviana wants to cradle fishes in her arms, wants to hear that clear day, that love cut short, that unchanging sky. Viviana is now Chile. She cradles fish under the sky that cries hosanna.

Surprising Christs fall in strange positions onto the crosses of the sea. Surprising baits rain from the sky: a last prayer rains, a last passion, a last day under the sky's hosannas. Infinite skies fall in strange positions onto the sea.

Infinite skies fall, infinite skies of broken legs, of arms bent against the neck, of heads twisted against backs. Skies weep downward falling in broken postures, in clouds of broken backs and broken skies. They fall, they sing.

That's your mother, there. That's your son.

That's your son. Viviana hears the arches of eyebrows incredibly raised, hears eyes endlessly open falling from the sky's eyebrows. Hears the nails sinking into the cross of the ocean. The whole Chilean sea is the cross. Infinite plains sing from the sky the hosanna of the cross which is the sea, of the food which falls like plains, like pieces of bread into the sacred stomach of the fish. Viviana hears infinite sacred shoals emerging, infinite fish singing with a voice taken from the sky.

The fish go up into the sky. Surprising baits rained down with surprising days, with images of almond trees, with loves cut short. Surprising baits rained on the sacred sea, on the sacred fish.

The sea is holy, holy the wide plains of human fruits that fall, the fish holy. I heard infinite days falling, bodies that fell with skies, with fields glimpsed between them, with trees like a chorus of crosses that sang out in song-sung waters.

Viviana cradles the holy sea. Viviana says somewhere in these sacred waters is her son.

Holy skies rained down. Infinities of water like children of the holy sky, yes, like pieces of bread, like holy baits beneath the ocean cross of Chile. They wept, rained down children of loves that never more, of endless meadows that fell in flames, of bushes that burn and do not burn up. Viviana hears whole skies fall like almond trees in flower, like pink cheeks in flower on the redeemed sea of Chile.

The bush that is the Chilean sea burns and does not burn up.

The holy plains of the sky burn falling. Human baits fall onto the flaming bush of the ocean. The fish swim up singing with the voice of the sky, shoals, infinities of fish rise up from the sacred waters.

Strange suns sing raining from the sky, strange fruits on the sacred ocean.

Fish in flames leap, amazing baits burn in the sea. Holy skies rained. Bushes of Chile, there are your sons. Bushes of Chile, there is the sea in flames.

See there the sea burning. Viviana hears skies burning among the flames of the sea, bushes that don't burn up, children of amazing bushes that burn without being consumed among the flaming waves. Strange days burn falling on the sea, amazing sacred baits that fall and sing upon the burnt pastures of the sea. Viviana is today Chile. She hears songs emerge from the water in flames, she hears the sacred sky burning with love upon the burning breakers. She hears the INRI of her love rise burning on the burning meadows of the Pacific.

She hears the INRI of the skies burning. Oceans and seas of Chile hear the INRI of the skies burning.

Surprising rose-blood baits rained from strange clouds over the sea, surprising incense-colored seas rise up now singing with the bait of the fish in the sky.

Listen to the song of the fish rising to the sky. Burning, the sacred ocean of Chile burning. Flames like incense tinge with blood and rose the burnt meadows of the Pacific.

Seas

Were thrown. Heavy with strange seed,
ploughed fields cover the sea.

Bruno Bends, Falls

In front the mountains emerge like a fine gauze that curves over the shadows. The snow of the cordillera phosphoresces lightly, like a gauze that floats. Above, the infinite stars and the black sky. Words are tenuous, the stars are tenuous.

I heard an unending field of white daisies. They bend in the wind. I hear the moaning of the thin stalks as they bend. It's a grating, high-pitched sound. When the wind stops the silence comes back.

Bruno. Only a white line that falls and rises again. Above the line everything is black and under it too. First there's the beach, I know, then the sea up to the horizon and then the sky. The night is a closed black box, underneath it the line of surf sounds and is white.

Bruno was my friend.

The cities are small and white in the night. In front there's the sea, only the white line of foam at its edge is visible. The sea, the thick darkness of the night.

I can hear the rabbit stunned by the headlights. Above, the snow on the mountains looks like a fine gauze that is going to fall on it and cover the small bloodstain that has started to show on its brown fur. The headlights shine on other places, other small coats of fur with blood on them.

A small red blood-spot covered by the snow gauze of all the mountains.

Susana is small.

The earth that covers Bruno is black. Bruno's face is white. But I don't know if it's earth or black water or black air. Susana's face is also white beneath the air or the water or the black earth.

I hear the sound of the daisies as they bend. Susana is a friend underneath the black field of white daisies.

The black sky sinks down into the sea, into the black field, into the gauze-like snow of the mountains. Up above, the stars bend in unison with the daisies in the wind. The stars make no sound, the stalks of the daisies cry out and I hear them.

Susana speaks words beneath the field or the water or the earth.

I remember a journey by sea. At the horizon the sky is infinitely diaphanous and I hear the silence and it becomes immense. Bruno was my friend. Susana is now thousands of Susanas. The silence takes me back to an asphalt road beside the mountains and the small rabbit, stunned and motionless. I stop and go back. There is a small blood-spot on its mouth, also on the fur at the neck, it weighs almost nothing in my hands. I hear the sound of the daisies as they bend.

It has almost no weight. Its lightly reddened incisors seem to screech at the moon. Susana has slightly red teeth. Her open mouth shows her slightly red teeth to the moon, like a screech.

In my imagination I write devastated love letters.

The front paws bent, pulled back against the slightly open mouth. Its tiny claws black with earth and then the incisors becoming red. Thousands of little incisors spotted with blood and the night. Thousands of letters full of love melting like a small fleck of blood under the gauze of snow, under the light gauze of snow wrapped around all the mountains.

Susana speaks words bent double under the land or the water or the black air. Under the earth of the tiny claws.

The little claws of the rabbit that's been run over. Its tiny claws and the hardened black earth behind them. Its eyes are earthy, like two small mounds of earth that grow in the black night. The sky is black, there are daisies. Its eyes buried under the bare earth that all the minuscule claws have gathered.

The gouged eye sockets. Bruno bends, falls.

The minuscule black claws and the brown fur. The white incisors are open, they are becoming red, gently. Behind, on its neck, the hairs stuck together with small patches of blood have gone rigid like barbs. I imagine the knife entering the neck, then the eyes. The knife moves up and down like the white line of surf in the thick darkness of the night. In my hands the little body bends. Bruno bends, falls.

In the night the stars bend like the daisies and the flecks of blood on the brown fur. The stalks of the daisies scream as they bend. The death blow and its almost weightless body bent double. The gauze of white snow on the mountains goes slightly red like the teeth under the tiny nose.

The teeth of hundreds of Susanas go slightly red beneath their lips, beneath the mouth of the night.

Ah, the sea, the sea beneath the night.

Bruno is dead. Susana is dead. The black land and beneath it the bloody gauze of the snow on the mountains. The white surf rises and falls in front. The small cities are white on the night roads. They are like flecks of light suddenly appearing and then nothing. Someone heard them and now they are thousands of white faces, with their teeth slightly reddened and the eye sockets empty. My love letters. Then nothing.

I pass through small towns in the night. I pass through fur flecked with blood. Both are tenuous. Bruno is tenuous. Susana now is tenuous.

Words of love are tenuous, as the night is tenuous, as the stalks of the daisies, yet they scream when the wind bends them. They scream and I hear them. My love letters are tenuous. They have small flecks of blood and saliva on them.

I am going back home, Bruno says. Susana also says she is going back home.

He bends, falls.

Bruno is a little black claw. Susana is a little
black claw. The daisies bend screeching. Here
are the daisies, the gauze snow on the
mountains. The line of surf.

I weep for a country that is my enemy.

The small white cities wait for Bruno, the small
white cities lit up by lamps in the night wait for
Susana. It's day, they're not there anymore and I
cry.

The Snow

Down below the mountain peak twists slowly
and bends. Hundreds of others further off do
the same: their sharp points, the rounded
mouths of the volcanoes. Behind there's the sea,
above, the tombstone of the sky. Below, the
huge cemetery of white mountains that twist
like needles bending.

Their bodies fall and twist. They look like
strange snowflakes against the immensity of
space. The white, pure snow will receive those
other bodies. It will receive them also. Below,
the white peaks, further back the line of the sea
and their bodies thrown like a strange snowfall.
Like strange snowflakes against the immense
crust.

It's them and they fall. It's a strange snowfall
coming down onto the white scar of the
mountains. There is also the sound of a strange
tenderness: snowflakes embraced by other snows,
small pieces of ice embraced by other ice.

It will speak also of a surprising and unexpected
country.

Fierce clouds snowed pink flakes, pink tombs.

Their snowflakes speak as they fall, as they snow on other snows. On the white gauze of the cordilleras. The snow will be pink in spring. The snow will be pink in the new spring.

Hundreds of tiny flowers tinged with the pink color of the new snowflakes, of the pink snows that speak as they melt in the thaw. Their flakes speak as they melt. They will reach the sea with the rivers, with the pink snow peaks of the mountains in the thaw.

Pink of all the snows, they say, it comes down through the light of the mountain.

Mauricio, Odette, María, Rubén. Are their names, but there are many more that also are their names. That also are a strange pink snowfall on the gauze of the mountains, on the snowflakes, on the small white flowers that grow at the bottom of the chasms of the cordilleras.

It's that. They are strange snowflakes, unusual flecks of a strange cloud that snowed reddening the gauze of the mountains. Of the peaks that go red with pink hail, with strange pink tear ducts snowed from a strange cloud.

They were thrown, they snow.

They fall on the tomb of all the pink snowflakes embraced by the snow of the mountains.

The bodies fall like small pieces of ice on the immense crust. There is the wind, then the soft embrace of its sister snows, its twin snows. The snow of the cordillera phosphoresces in the night as it bends. It phosphoresces with them also.

Now they are strange flakes of pink snow that the sister snows embrace. That the gullies of the cordilleras embrace. That the thousands of white flowers that grow in the chasms of the cordilleras embrace.

It's that. Night, the pink snow, the white flowers down in the chasms. Their bodies snow. They are strange snowflakes that fall, strange pieces of snow or hail that fall in the rose-pink night of the mountains.

Mauricio, Odette, María, Rubén. The small flowers take on the pink color of that snowfall.

Hundreds of mountains twist as they make rose-colored hail that the light of the stars passes through. Hundreds of minuscule petals, of little tombs of snowflakes that the dawn stars pass through. Small snowflakes that are transparent tombs the rose light of dawn passes through.

Now they are snowflakes pierced by the rose-blood color of the stars. They all lie there. The light passes through them like another snow-field, like other strange tears that spring brought.

It's that. The thaw brings down rose ice particles from the snow of the mountains. There is a day of snow that dawns with the color of the minuscule rose snowflakes of all the mountains. With the pink color of the thaw.

Of the new blood-red color of the thaw that passes through the minuscule dead snowflakes of the spring.

The pink underside of the eyelids. It's the rose-pink inside of the tear ducts when they weep. They were thrown and now they are lumps of pink snow embraced by the fine gauze that phosphoresces on the cordilleras. Tomorrow the thaw will come and they will hear the pity of the mountains, they will hear the pink bandage of snow that weeps from the blood-colored tear ducts of all the mountains, of all the rivers and thaws.

The pink snow of blood, the open tear ducts that stain the minuscule flowers cramped to the chasms of blood that lie between the peaks.

Mauricio, Odette, María, Rubén lie there. They embrace each other.

Their sounds embrace. They lie embracing each other like other snowflakes with the snow, like other pieces of ice with the ice. The sound of the rose blood that falls phosphorescing like the tear ducts behind the cordillera.

They lie in all the tombs our country offers them.

They threw them. The tear ducts are red from crying. The night is red in the blood chasms of the bandaged cordilleras. They hear their snowflakes bandage the red night and the pink waters of the thaw come down. They hear the sky coming down with all the strange hail fallen on the red gauze of the mountains.

The bandaged mountains. Fierce clouds of snow flew over the cordilleras.

Strange clouds from a country where the snows embrace tiny red flecks, small broken red hail-stones. Embrace the insides of all the chasms of white and pink flowers that phosphoresce in the bandaged night of the mountains. The great snowfalls embrace. It's that. Hundreds of snowflakes that fall embracing the thousands of little rose-pink tombs that the spring brings down.

It's hundreds of tombs that come down embracing all the pink flowers of the thaw.

The stars. The stars are there. They are like the thousands of white flowers that grow at the bottom of black chasms. The stars are white like the minuscule snowflakes, the tear ducts are red when there is crying. The stars also become pink before dawn. Mauricio, Odette, María, Rubén. Are there, are now like flakes of snow. The tear ducts become red when there is crying.

They all lie there. The stars turn pink at the end of the night. The snowflakes of these tombs are pink at the end of the night.

It is dawn of a country not heard, the red crown of stars of a nation never heard. Thousands of stars before dawn. Hundreds of red hailstones before they melt in the cradle of other snows in the thaw. Here is love, they say, it is said to them.

It is love, they say. It is said to them of that rose-pink color tomb of the stars.

Down below, the cemetery of the crusted mountains which twist. Up above, the pink tear ducts of the stars, the stars before dawn. The tear ducts of the stars are pink like letters soaked in blood. Like letters that melt into small flecks of blood like the snow, like the phosphorescent gauze of all the mountains.

Mauricio, Odette, María, Rubén. Now they are hundreds of pink tombs on the gauze of the mountains. Here is love, they say, they say to them, it is love which comes down with all the pink snowflakes that the new spring takes to the sea. We speak of a new spring, of a new country that no one had conceived.

We speak, they say to them, the things that the snows speak, that the snowed cordilleras speak. Of snowflakes that are minuscule tombs that speak as they come down in the thaws in the night encaged in flowers that is the rose-pink night of the stars.

We speak, they say, of a new country, a new love that no one had conceived.

It hailed, strange hailstones came down, strange eyelids upon the needles of the cordilleras. Mauricio, Odette, María, Rubén. They are hundreds of pink eyelids, of pink cheeks and cheekbones snowing down from furious clouds, hundreds of melting snowflakes embracing each other in the reddened tear ducts of the cordilleras. They threw them all down, they disemboweled them. The blood color of dawn is like the reddened blood color of tear ducts when they cry.

Mauricio, Odette, María, Rubén. They hailed down on an unexpected tenderness, on a rose-pink snow dawn that embraced the little broken flakes of gusting snow, that embraced the hundreds of rose-pink tombs of ice that snowed down.

They are there, in an unheard country where the peaks embrace strange little pieces of ice fallen from fierce clouds. Dawn is there and the pink blood color of the sky embracing all the tombs that snowed onto the crusted peaks. They are small pink snowflakes suckled by the sky blood color gauze that dawns over the mountains.

They threw them all down. Their fierce rose-pink stuck like never before to life.

In the snow

The tear ducts are pink when there is crying.

The Desert

Down below, the endless stones of the desert, mountains of stones, long escarpments of stones, infinite stones on the desert like a sea. The sky above, the blue sky falling. The stones cry out as they smash into the air, into the sky that's falling.

The desert cries out. There's a limestone wall with names. There's a white wall and little bottles with plastic flowers that cry out as they bend in the wind.

A little further off there's a ship. No one would say there can be a ship in the middle of the desert. It's a big, rusty ship, lying on the stones. No one would say it could be, but it's there. The same sky that falls on the stones falls on the ship. All the stones cry out.

They cry out, the Chilean desert cries out. No one would say this could be, but they cry out.

There's a ship in the middle of the desert. A ship lying on the stones of the desert and above, the sinking tombstone of the sky. The inverted ocean of the sky falls on the stones and they cry out. No one except stones can cry out like that. Mireya covers her ears so as not to hear the screeching of the desert. Chile cries out, the Chilean desert cries out. Mireya gathers small plastic flowers in front of a ship that's beached on the mounds of stones.

Here are the coasts, the obdurate sealess coasts climbing backward up the dead waves of the mountains.

Mireya says she is the mother of Chile. That she is the mother of a ship lying in the middle of the desert.

From far off it looks like a black stain, but it's a ship. Below it the stones piled up against the hull seem like waves. But they are not waves, they are only stones and they cry out. The breakers cry out as they rear up. The sun also is sinking and colored plastic flowers like tiny suns. Here is the sea of the desert, the sea of stones of the desert boiling in front of Chile.

Here are the little flowers and the gangrenous coasts of the dry empty sea.

Mireya gives a name to each one of these flowers. Against the ship they look like tiny suns saying goodbye to it.

The desert cries out, the desiccated port cries out, the sea of stones cries out whipped by the wind. Mireya places flowers for the crew of a black rusty ship. Each flower has a name and they bend together like handkerchiefs saying goodbye. Mireya says she is the mother of a ship of the disappeared beached in the desert. She says the ship is Chile, that it used to be a ship of living people but that it now cuts through the sea of stones with its dead children.

The flowers bend. Waves and waves of stones smash against the sides of a rusty hull.

There is a dry empty port and a ship with a crew of dead people aground in the middle of the desert. Mireya says they are her children. The sea of stones cries out.

Chile runs aground and sinks in the dry stony slopes of the waves.

In the desert nights there's mist, but now there's sun. The stones boil under the sun and crash against the rusty hull. The immobile ship seems to be sinking. No one would say a ship can sink in the middle of the desert, but it's sinking. In the night the mist will come, but now there's sun.

There is a cross. There is a black rusty ship wrecked on the stones.

Who would say a country with a cross sinking in the desert. Who would say the night buried in the middle of the day. Who a tomb sunk in the middle of a day full of sun.

The night sinks in the middle of the day. Mireya says that there's a ship full of dead people sinking in the desert.

A country of the disappeared is shipwrecked in the desert. The prow of dead landscapes sinks wrecked like the sun on the stones. The sun shines down on a black stain in the middle of the day. In the distance it seems just like a stain, but it's a ship in bright sunlight burying itself with its night in the stony fields of the desert. *If they keep silent the stones will cry out.*

Mireya says that they all kept silent and that is why the stones of the desert cry out. That they cry out, and the flowers also are small stones crying out as they bend before a ship of dead people.

The ship sinks. The arid breakers pile up falling on Chile and screech, the waves screech, the earthy sea screeches. Mireya puts flowers for the crew of a nation of dead people run aground in the middle of the desert. She says that the silence of all was the tomb and that this is why the stones cry out covering the dead ship of these lands.

A sea of dead is sinking among the stones. The sun going down lights up a night that descends upon the sepulcher of the desert. Here is the stain like a grave in the earth. The ship descends, the dead landscapes descend while the stone-capped waves close over them and cover them. Here is the night in the middle of the day, here are the stones that cry out.

Here is the night mist of the desert sinking in the middle of the day. The dead ship sinks under the mist of stones and the stones screech. Chile is shipwrecked and the dry sea closes over it, the waves of stones close over it and cry out.

The black rusty night sinks crying out in the desert.

A ship of disappeared sinks and the dead rocks close over it and screech. Mireya covers her ears and puts plastic flowers in front of the grave of the dead coasts, of the dead night, of her disappeared children dead in the stone oceans of the Atacama Desert.*

* A six-hundred-mile desert strip extending between the sea and the Andes, from the north of Santiago to the border of Peru. —*Trans.*

It is wrecked, it is sinking. The rusty ship sinks and the desert closes over it and covers it. The desert closes over it and Chile sinks, the dead cornice of the Pacific sinks, the dead prow of the landscapes sinks while the stones that fall onto them cry out that nothing is alive, that nothing lives anymore, that if one died for all all are dead.

The dead sand dunes close, the tomb of the dead landscapes closes.

The dry waves close. Mireya says there's a ship in a dustbowl of dead people. That it's there, that once there used to be a country, but that now it's just a ship covered over by the dead sea of its landscapes.

She says that if one died for all all the dead seas are one, the dead coasts are one, the crying stones are one and that silence is the rock that closed the sepulcher of the landscapes. She says that one died for all and that is why even the stones are the body that cries out while the dead plains are nailed onto Chile.

Everything has finished. The black rusty hull disappears in the sea of stones. The sky falls on top of them and they cry out. There is a white wall with names across it and plastic flowers underneath. There is a plain and the dry breakers of the sky that come falling like a dustheap of dead on the sepulcher of the landscapes. Everything has finished. Mireya says that everything finally is finished.

The rippled breakers fall, the dead sea falls like a pile of earth. The dead landscapes fall like seas of earth.

There is a ship of disappeared and dead and on top of it the stones of the desert. There is a white limestone wall with names on it and behind it the ocean of earth falling onto the last flat surfaces. Mireya says that everything is finished and she leaves small plastic flowers on the surface of the field of stones that is dying, she says that it is the last sea and it is dying.

That they are the last stones on a ship of dead and they are dying. That Chile is dying. That you yourself are the last cry that is dying under the final INRI of the landscapes.

In memoriam

There is a ship in the desert. Who would say
that this can be, but there is a black rusty ship
sunk in the desert.

II

There laid they Jesus therefore ... for the sepulcher was nigh at hand.

— JOHN 19:42

I feel you, I touch you, and the tips of my fingers, accustomed always to follow yours*

*In the original edition, this phrase is printed in braille.—*Trans.*

The Descent

I touch your skin, your body, and the tips of my fingers, which always used to follow yours, sense in the darkness that we are descending. They have destroyed all the bridges and the cordilleras are sinking, the Pacific is sinking, and its remains are sinking in front of us as the remains of our heart also sink. In the face of death somebody said something to us about resurrection. Does that mean your empty eye sockets will see? That my fingertips will go on touching yours? My fingers touch your fingers in the darkness and go down as now the peaks, the sea go down, as our dead love, our dead gaze, these dead words go down. Like a field of daisies that bend I touch your skin, your body, and my hands try to find in the darkness the skin of snow in which we may perhaps live again. But no, of the peaks of the Andes only the traces of these words remain, of these dead pages, of a wide, dead field of flowers where the cordilleras like white shrouds, with us beneath them and still embracing, are sinking down.

The line of the cordillera breaks away from the sky and sinks, slowly sinks, separates from the sky and sinks. It's common for cordilleras to sink, it's common to hear the snows descending, to hear the peaks of mountains break away and fall. In an enemy country it's a common thing to hear mountains of bodies sinking heads down. The Andes sink into the sea of stones. Bruno waits under the stones. Susana also waits for the mountains and mountains of bodies under the stones.

The frozen mountains collapse onto themselves and fall. Maybe the sea receives them. Maybe there is a sea where the frozen bodies fall. Maybe, Zurita, that is the sea. A limbo where bodies fall. There will also be daisies. Daisies at the bottom of the sea, at the bottom of the sea of stones. Maybe the daisies love the frozen mountains. Maybe the chained bodies can hear them groan. In an enemy country it's common for the daisies to groan as they hear the cordilleras fall.

The Pacific breaks away from the coastline and falls. First it was the cordilleras and now it is the sea that falls. From the coast to the horizon it falls. In an enemy country it is common for bodies to fall, for the sea to break away from the coast and fall like the daisies that groan as they hear the cordilleras sinking where love, where maybe love, Zurita, moans and weeps because in an enemy country it is common for the Pacific to collapse face down like a broken torso on the stones.

The Andes are dead stars at the bottom of the sea of stones. The Pacific also is a dead star at the bottom of the sea of stones. Under the stones the sepulcher of the sea and of the cordilleras is like a night thick with daisies and dead stars. The dead stars of the Andes and of the Pacific cross at the bottom of the stones. The daisies bend in front of the cross and moan. In an enemy country it is a common thing for stars to form a cross over our dead faces.

The Pacific Ocean broke away from the horizon and lies beneath the stones, the cordillera of the Andes also lies there. The stones cover the peaks and the sea like a black field. The daisies of the black fields, of the black earth or water, bend and groan over the collapsed mountains, over the fallen sea. In an enemy country it is common for the ocean and the mountains to lie beneath the stones, that love should lie there, that your love, Zurita, should lie there and that your blind eyes should be a tomb embracing them.

The mountains embrace at the bottom, the sea is of stones and they embrace. Maybe the mountains and the sea are sleeping. In an enemy country it is common for fallen bodies to embrace as if sleeping. Infinite fields of daisies descend to the edge of the beach where the Pacific was before. Other fields do the same where the cordilleras were. The cordilleras and the sea lie down below and embrace each other. In an enemy country it is a common thing for the sea and the mountains to embrace lying face down as if they were asleep.

We hear the sea falling, the peaks, the plains and it was our blind bodies that collapsed and piled up under the stones. The daisies groan and maybe they are the fingers that feel us and touch in us the emptied coasts. Maybe it is a common thing for flowers. In an enemy country maybe it is common for daisies to bend over and touch us in the collapsed sea. In an enemy country perhaps the daisies as they climb touch the mountains with their fingers.

Here under the stones the cordilleras of the Andes and the Pacific lie embraced. The daisies grow in the spring. Perhaps the spring may grow. Perhaps the mountains and the ocean may rise up from their embrace beneath the stones and the daisies will be the new spring. Bruno, Susana, perhaps their bodies may rise up from under the stones. In an enemy country it is a common thing for daisies to hold the snow that is left by bodies which fell in spring.

I touch your flesh, your skin, and the tips of my
fingers search for yours because if I love you and
you love me perhaps not everything is lost. The
mountains sleep below and perhaps the daisies
light up the field of white flowers. A field where
the Andes and the Pacific embracing under the
dead earth wake up and our blind eyes emerging
in the new spring become like a horizon of
flowers. Will it be? Will it be like this? The daisies
continue bending over the sea which is dead, over
the great peaks which are dead and in the darkness,
having come down, like two emptied skins that
seek each other my fingers grope to touch yours
because if I touch you and you touch me perhaps
not everything is lost and we can still know
something of love. Of all the dead loves we were
and of a field of flowers that will grow when our
white shrouds, when our shrouds of the snow of
all the sunken mountains kiss us as we lie face
down and turn our bristling eyelashes upward.

I feel you, I touch you, and the tips of my fingers,
seek yours because if I*

---

*In the original edition, this phrase is printed in braille.— *Trans*.

III

Peace be unto you.

—JOHN 20:41

Flowers

A face is a face in a desert in flower. I hear wide plains flower, I heard whole deserts cover themselves with flowers. A flower is a face in the solitude of the desert as a face is a flower in the solitude of things. A face hears years, seasons, endless lives that finish. A flower just a few days, a few twilights, a few endless nights that finish. A face is another flower that finishes. I heard infinite deserts that had come into flower destroyed. I'm called Zurita and I tell you these things just like I could tell you others. Maybe the demented flowers love one another.

The Chilean desert. There's a ship in the middle of the desert and a woman leaving flowers beside it. The stones cry out. No one except stones can cry out like that. The flowers also cry out, but only when the wind bends them. I heard whole fields of flowers bending in the wind.

They gouged out their eyes, did you know that? They tore their eyes from the sockets. That is why in these poems no one sees, they only hear. The flowers hear and sometimes cry out when they bend in the wind. The faces do not see. The stones are mad and only cry out.

No one sees. Maybe the sickled flowers love one another.

I heard the wide horizons of the east being emptied, I heard the Andes disappear. I heard huge white magnolias take the place of the mountains. They were mountains, now they are flowers. Enormous white magnolias are now where the cordillera was. The horizon is flowers, the cordillera of the Andes is now white magnolias that moan. I love you, they moan. For the first time, since the beginning of the world, what the cordilleras never told us the flowers are now telling us. The flowers which are where the Andes were tell us they love us.

The Pacific disappeared and in its place flowers grew. Infinite blue hydrangeas cover the expanses where the sea once was. Infinite flowers groan as the wind shakes them. The sea is a cemetery, the flowers groan while another sky grows above them. The magnolias of the east where the cordilleras were and the hydrangeas of the west where the sea was speak to each other and to us. From the thorns of Chile they tell us of a passion which neither the cordilleras nor the sea ever told us of. Blue hydrangeas now cover the immense territories of the Pacific.

I heard the horizons east and west transformed into flowers: I heard the endless glaciers, blind oceans, icebergs from other worlds floating among the flowers of the Pacific. I heard crowns of thorns come into flower and tell you that all the hydrangeas of the east and the magnolias of the west are your own body in flower. From your empty eye sockets Chile's cross of thorns rose upwards and the sky rising up from the perforated cavities of your eyes was like a field of lilies. Then I heard incredible horizons, peaks made of flowers, whole seas of snow going upward and flowering. Out of the crowns of thorns of your eyes. Did they empty your eye sockets? Did they gouge them out? As if you could see again roses rise up out of your empty eye sockets amazed rose trees the smell of the sea.

Then the flowers of the Andes and the flowers
of the Pacific say they love us. That is what they
say to us: that they love us. The marvelous
acacias with yellow flowers rising up out of all
the blood of the fields and the acacias that now
grow where the narrow plains were say it. And
they say it to you, murderers, destroyers of
human beings, the marvelous acacias in the
fields and the magnolias that grow where the
cordilleras used to be and the bluish hydrangeas
that grow where the Pacific once was say it.
Listen little dove all the flowers of the deserts,
of the seashores of Chile and mountains, love us.
I died and they love me. You died and they love
you. Yes snowflower of the plains they say
*vidalitay** my little dove, the flowers which are where the
ocean was, the cordilleras and valleys are telling
us they love us.

* Author's note: Or *vidala*: A type of folk song, with roots in native Andean
music, found in Argentina, Uruguay, and Chile.

There then are the graveyards of Chile:
geraniums, fields of sunflowers of the stars,
magnolias that flame where the Andes used
to be, the narrow strip of deserts and beaches
that will be rose trees floating on the sea. They
are the graveyards of flowers, the horizon of the
cordilleras rising out of your empty eye sockets,
because the blinded mountains and the blind
snows and the peaks of Chile are the flowers that
cover the dead craters of your eyes. When the
distant auroras and the dawns receive into them-
selves the dismembered legs that fell, the torsos,
the backs that fell, they rose up and it was your
emptied eye sockets that filled with geraniums
like the whole sky that was born yes, little dove,
graveyards of geraniums your eyes fields of stars
the sunflowers in flower.

The graveyards are the sky of flowers of Chile
and the empty tombs of your eyes are the hollow
places where the Pacific now flowers. And the
blind graves that heard your eyes being torn out
are now the sky full of flowers that tells us of a
love that is alive. The daisies of that living love
are in the sky and all the mountains and stars are
like moons of geraniums and the immense
morning stars rolling like balls of fire in the rose-
pink dawn were flowers also. Then I heard your
love and my devastated love rising upward and
floating above the glaciers and I loved your love
on the long snowfields of white flowers. Are you
there? Is it you? and your eyelids rise from the
stones in flower and cover the horizon with
white flowers, the glaciers with white flowers,
the trembling stars with white flowers. Are your
eyes alive? Your torn-out eyes? And all dawn long
it is white flowers answering us when the sky
falls onto us and we cry.

Then the cordilleras disappeared, the Pacific dis-
appeared and all Chile now is flowers. Infinite
white magnolias the Andes, infinite hydrangeas
the ocean and endless flowers the narrow strip
of the plains. Yes, yellow balsam, narcissi in the
mouth of the volcanoes and the long riverbeds
in flower, the flowers telling us what neither sky
nor sea nor earth ever told us and the fields of
rose trees growing out of our dead eyes were
like beaches rising up in the air. When the
Pacific disappeared and the bluish hydrangeas
came up, when the cordilleras sank and white
flowers emerged above them, then they erased
the sky and the sky covered over with flowers
opened the graves that were our faces, buried,
empty, suspended over Chile like geraniums.
Then the giant sunflowers of the stars, the
hydrangeas of the ocean, the magnolias of the
Andes speak to us, because what neither the
mountains, the Pacific, not the stars ever told us
they tell us now, but imagine, little dove, your
flowers.

And they love us, and they tell us they love us.
The flowers moving in the wind, little dove,
vidala, tell us they love us. And the graveyards
of Chile tell us they love us and the flowers say
your blind love that rises up with my blind love
scattered over the white fields of the glaciers.
When they tore out our eyeballs with hooks and
the flowers began to grow out of the blinded
hooks. When they piled us on top of each other
and threw us into the blinded Pacific, into the
blinded volcanoes, onto the whole long blinded
country and the red sky was flowers we heard
coming out as we lay dying. Yes, a face is a face
in the deserts in flower and the new oceans, the
new peaks and deserts that cried out with the
stones the love of all the flowers that love us
were the sky above our faces. And they love us,
and they said to us then, *vidalitay*, that they love
us because a desert is a desert is a face come
into flower, and the sky has our faces stuck to it,
flowering out of the whole desert like a graveyard
the whole of Chile with flowers of you with
flowers who were dying of you with flowers the
morning.

A face is your face a desert in flower. The
severed flowers love one another. A face loved
is a flower in the desert just as the desert is
night for the flowers. They gouged out their eye
sockets, did you know that? They severed their
eyes. The severed flowers groan and our dead
faces flower in the desert because a face is a
face in the brevity of things just as the flowers
are a desert in the brevity of the night. When
flowers are the night and the night the blinded
love that loves us.

A desert is then a desert a dream come into
flower and your blind dead face rises up and is
covered with rose trees because the flowers love
us and the flowers are nights of our blind love
rising up above the severed skies.

And the flowers love us, yes, Zurita, they love
us, and severed they grow from your blind eyes
to say to us the love our countries never said to
us, when the sky grew in your emptied night
and the whole sky was your face full of flowers
rising upward.

Because the flowers love us. Because the severed
flowers love us. Because the dead flowers, Zurita,
love us.

Oh yes

Oh yes the entire horizon then said to us, the
living flowers love us.

Breakers

The ocean waves float across the sky. The Pacific, the beaches. From down below it looks like winds, but they're ocean waves moving across the sky. Viviana listens to endless oceans rise upward and she also rises upward. Her son also rises upward with the rose-pink snow peaks of the cordilleras. The snow-pink blood of the cordilleras and the blood-covered waves of the returning seas float suspended over the sky. The snow peaks also float, the sea, the mountains.

All the bodies thrown into the mountains, rivers, and sea of Chile float on the wind. They have been returned to the sky and they float.

Waves have come back again, tidewaters have come back again and swim over the wind. Mountains and mountains rise upward floating, cordilleras and cordilleras of bodies return spread out like blood-colored lava of all the volcanoes, of all the mountains and snow peaks. The ocean waves of resurrection float in the sky and are the sea.

A sea. They say a new sea. Oh yes they say a new sky.

Let us speak then of the flight of the new ocean
and of the breakers in the sky. Of bodies thrown
out over the volcanoes, rivers, and lakes of Chile
and that now are the sea and return. Of the love
from which we were murdered and which now
returns. Of the life which returns and of the
hailstones of you and me embracing each other
over the snowfields. Of the meat for fish that we
were and of the Pacific because the Pacific was
resurrection and the breakers of resurrection
beat and thrashed against the mountains.

And it was the floating cordilleras and the
thrown hailstones that we were, the soft bait
for fish that we were when our blind eyes heard
the waves become dumb and the breakers of
resurrection were the mute dream that for love
tore off our dead flesh.

Listen now to the waves thrashing against the peaks, the new beaches that had not been dreamt of because the breakers float over the sky and are a sea. And the thrown bodies float over the sky and are a sea and the clouds of death open to show us the unclouded mountains and are a sea. And the multitude of their still broken torsos is a sea and the cordilleras and cordilleras of their bodies floating like the resurrection over the blazing waters are the waves.

Upon the waves, upon the beaches that were raising up a new country that had not been contemplated when love, when our empty eyes turned upward and we heard the mountain peaks tremble and it was the whole resurrection crashing against the sky like new waves against the mountains.

Yes, because the breakers suddenly went silent and the empty eye sockets heard the silence of the sea and the dawn rising out of the sea lit up our disappeared bodies weeping to each other beneath the morning. When the tidewaters went upward until they were suspended over the massacred Andes and crying out, crying out as we lay face down, we heard the waves of resurrection rolling over the peaks and like hard black fields our eyes heard us throb like beetles crawling up the foaming mountains.

Yes, when everything went silent and those thrown out over Chile placed their feet once more on the snow and the snow that received the weight of their new limbs creaked like a sea. And we wept believing we were rising upward and our eyes went on hearing us like someone who hears a sea appear in the morning and it wasn't the sea yet but a dream of the sea in the morning.

Yes, because thrown out of the sky we heard the silence of the breakers and the roar of the mute breakers beat like a hurricane against the cordilleras like wind on fields of grass. And wind upon wind, field upon field, the dawn emerging from the sea tore at our dry eyelids and the mute snow of the mountains, the mute ocean, the mute dawn, wept to hear the breakers of resurrection, immobile, hardened, as if still waiting a split second more before they fell singing on top of our dead bodies.

And the mute mountains rose up on top of the mountains. And the silent breakers rose upon the breakers when the Andes became a single thing with the sea which floated suspended over our faces and faces and foam and death piled up beneath us as if a wave of light had broken and was singing in our eyes.

And then rained down from ferocious clouds
our empty pupils heard the suspended breakers
beat while down below our legs, arms, torsos
moved about like small waves without life
waiting for the final roar of their waters.
Because they threw us into the sea and the fish
were the carnivorous tombs of the sea. Because
they threw us into the volcanoes and the craters
were the carnivorous tombs of the volcanoes.
Yes, because they killed us and we died and the
breakers of resurrection glided above us like
immense shattered ice floes about to smash
down on our own dead waves.

And then, like vast blocks of ice crashing down,
I heard the tumult and you heard it and the
foam made by the blocks of ice as they crashed
into the sea exploded upward and the breakers
of resurrection beat above us like a furious flock
of birds that descended upon us pecking us oh
yes death, oh yes tidewaters, oh yes Viviana.

And then, on fire, as if the whole Pacific were burning, the breakers flashed and the glow of the waves over the horizon dyed the sky with the ancient red color of our flesh. When the waves soaked us and the skies made us seasick carrying us upward. When sobbing among the flames of the waters we felt ourselves move once again and it was all the seas, all the lakes and rivers, all the deserts and mountains burning into the sky as if the whole ocean were on fire as it became with us alive again and these waves were setting on fire our flesh with love.

Our sea burns. Burns without consuming itself.

Listen then to the tumult of the sea burning on the horizon. The Pacific is burning and Viviana sings with the cheeks of our love, with the new cheekbones of our love, with the resurrection of our love flying up into the sky like the flames of a dream flickering before us.

Listen then to the waves burning. Amazing baits float on the flames and rise upward. The breakers of Chile burn and sing, bushes of water crackle under the burning skies of the ocean. Whole burning days, sunny mornings, fields barely glimpsed rise now singing between the flames of the Pacific. *And death found no place.*

The Pacific burns, the breakers of the resurrection burn over the Chilean sky.

Surprising baits, amazing human fruits become whole again singing. Incredible fish fly over the burning ocean. Infinite fish that ascend with sunny days in their mouth, with loves brought back, with fragments of ribs now changed. Incredible fish rise up from the flames of the burning sea and sing with the voice of the sky. The waves sing on the salvaged beaches. They burn above the sky and sing.

Viviana hears human meadows rise again between flames, days that return, fruits like suns that rise up restored over the flatlands of the sea. Viviana hears her son ascend out of the salvaged waves.

Salvaged baits that return from the sea.

Oh yes, they say

Salvaged, oh yes they say salvaged as the flowers
sometimes say.

Bruno, Susana

The small white cities wait for Bruno, the small cities lit up in the night wait for Susana. It is remembered that it is day now, the sea is remembered.

Of the light then and of the roar of the sea in the
light that hits us inside the eyes because the
empty sockets of our eyes are the sea's. Of all the
light then and of the snowfields which are our
blind faces imprinted, blown, falling upward
with all the living cheeks of our dead cheeks,
with the living arms of our dead arms, with all
the waves exploding with the sound forever of
our names and of the living ocean that speaks
forever to us above the cordilleras.

When we heard the sea without end and even
the stones shouted out our names.

When they touched us with love and the
breakers and the snow of the breakers sounded
our names and we got up out of our sleep to
the sound of our dead names, raising our new
arms to them in a living dream.

To the love which rose through us making the
hairs on our arms stand on end and the hairs
were the wheat fields forever that grew waving
out of all the tombs of earth where we fell. Like
love and all that is dead which lives and
returns like the dream of the sky that returns
and is the light forever of the sea.

Bruno remembers a sea and Susana also
remembers. There is light from the mountains
and the eyes forever of all the white towns,
of all the white cheeks stretched like bandages
over the bloodied cheekbones of the cordilleras.
The little towns are white in the wind and now
their faces hear a white town down below and
sing. There is the light like the white gauze of
the cordilleras in the sky. There is the sea and
the white line of the breakers that sing, the
tombs of their eyes and of the sea that sing.

They hear a white town down below and sing.
Bruno's gouged eyes sing. Susana's emptied eyes
sing.

They are thousands of white towns and they
sing. Thousands of Susanas, thousands of
Brunos in the gauze of the snow peaks. Their
cheeks cover the cheekbones of the mountains
and dream in the white wind, in the white
bandages. The bloodied bandages of the
cordilleras fall open in the sky and are white.

Oh yes, Bruno, oh yes, Susana. The bloodied
bandages fall open in the sky and are white.

There is the bandage crossed by light that is the Andes and above, the written sky, the sea forever. The hollow of the ocean opens and our faces hear their names rise over them. They will rise up. The graves will open like a sea and our country will be another country of seas surging upward. The snows open and the landscapes emerge once again imprinted on the horizon. On the living oceans of all the horizons. Of all the sky forever rising through the illuminated hollows of your eyes.

The Andes open. The gauze of the snow peaks opens in the illuminated sky and is your eyes.

And the tombs that remained of the snow open and the white cordilleras hear us rise up because we are the ocean that rises. When the hollows of the sky like mouths of light shouted our names to us and our dead names were written singing over the living horizons.

There are flowers alive with light and the Pacific.
There are flowers and all the flowers of a dream.
There are the names of our dead names and the
flowers stuck like another sea to the living sky.
Like another living snow to the dead snows
when the dead and living cordilleras forever
repeated our names, calling us, because the
whole sky sings over the living earth on which
they killed us. Us dead and alive. Us dead and
alive rising like pieces of snow forever and the
sky.

There are the flowers, the Pacific forever and
above, the eyelids of the sky.

When the eyelids of the sky opened showing us
our white eyes and as in a dream where no one
dies we heard the song of the dead who went on
calling us by our living names. By the living love
that shouts "look" to us. And there is the living
sky looking at us.

Smashed to pieces by light the stones ascend above the sky and embrace one another. They ascend and sing. There is a ship in the middle of the desert and thousands of flowers that cover its hull and sing. She hears the flowers cover the stones of the desert and rise upward infinitely above the desert. Above the cross of the cheek-bones and white torsos that cry out to the sky and rise upward singing like an illuminated sea that embraced itself over the mountains.

They sing, their torsos, their white cheekbones sing as they rise upward with the light of the mountains.

Thousands of cheekbones and torsos embrace rising upward over the flowers of the desert and sing. The cross of their faces rises like a dream stuck to the ocean and sings. She hears the Pacific Ocean rise up above the sky in flower, above the INRI in flower of the Atacama Desert.

Bruno says he has gone back home. Susana also says she has gone back home. Then there is the light and the bandaged peaks of the sky. There is the horizon and the gauze made of light of the small white towns on the peaks. The bloodied bandages of the Andes are white and their faces hear the houses in the small towns going white like flecks of blood in the snow. There are the snows, there is the sky. Bruno and Susana hear the houses of their small white towns rise up in the bandaged sky of the mountains.

There is the light of the cordilleras and the houses of their small white towns in the snow gauze.

Bruno says he has come home. Susana also says it. The white towns of the white air or water or land rise upward like small flecks of blood evaporated in the snow. There is the snow, the blue of the sky. The bandages made of light of the sky over their houses in the snowfields.

Bruno, Susana. In my mind I write devastated love letters.

Clothed in light, as in a dream, the demented
landscapes and the flight forever of your
cordilleras rose in the transparent morning as
my cheekbones of love grew transparent
ascending in yours. And my cheeks of love
became transparent in your cheeks and the eyes
that were dust of the whole of death, of the
whole dream thrown, heard the day emerge
sticking to them like faces forever over the
illuminated cheekbones of the mountains.

And the plains were illuminated in the plains.
And the winds were aroused in the winds.

And the flaming beaches burned on the beaches
and the faces of the whole of love fell on our
dead faces and their flight kissed us like the
winds forever over the fields.

And forever, and like faces and fields forever,
and like the whole of dreaming and death
forever, the final cordilleras were in flame and
the plains ascended becoming transparent like
demented cheeks and forever over the quaking
skies of morning.

Forever?

Then a whole snowfall of names comes into memory: Paulina, Mireya, Viviana. Have they seen Susana? Have you seen Bruno?

A Path in the Solitudes

And very slowly, like an ocean whose waters begin to stir, we emerged onto the plains and the plains seemed like waves as they heaved with the movement of our bodies.

Yes, because the sky and the cordilleras will be in flame, the deserts and beaches will open their solitudes and our broken bodies will traverse their solitude, will walk again on the grass and the movements of our bodies as they walk on the plains will seem like a sea that begins to stir.

Because our corpses will live again. Yes, because our bodies will live again, and the sky in flame will be a sea of grass that hears our footsteps again. And a sea will open in the solitudes.

And then a path will be traced in the solitudes and like two lovers who wake up together our eyes as they look up will once again unite the horizons with the glaciers, the peaks with the chasms, the empty mouths of the volcanoes with the ocean and our new pupils as they flood the silenced beaches will be like rivers giving water to the desert. The white crests of the Andes will join with the Pacific, like waves breaking upward our stiffened eyelids will open and like a sea rising up in the solitudes the earth will give up its dead.

And the sea emerged out of our dead bodies and
the sky domed with flowers rose up out of our
dead cheekbones, out of the twisted stones, out
of the face of our dead faces, and the ocean of
the sky was the dream that our eyes as they
opened raised up in front of us. Are you alive? Is
it possible? And like two children just born our
lips began to move again over our fallen
mouths, over the rim of our teeth, over our col-
lapsed cheeks that stuck to us again like the
whole horizon that stuck to us, exactly that, the
air pushing again through our pink throats.

And then the jubilation blowing upon us, like
all the breath blowing upon our flesh-colored
flesh, my joy rose up with your joy and the
jubilation of our faces as they rose made the
plains ripple and the plains were like the buds of
flowers pushing us out of our soaked cadavers.

And the new mountains occupying the place of
the seas and the new seas occupying the place of
the mountains rose up and their limbs rose up
like fields of grass over the reddened sky. And
the reborn arms and torsos, the torn-off legs
covered the fields like clouds moving over grass.
And it was the sea of the Andes rising and the
peaks of the Pacific were the whole of light
ascending, flashing onto the cordilleras and the
empty hollows of their eyes were rising upward
and it was the ocean in flame over the mountains
that filled the hollows of their eyes.

And jumping together, like seas and mountains
dancing, like hills dancing, we heard ourselves
risen to our feet and it was the infinite sky,
risen, lightly touching us with all the things that
rise upward, the day, sleep, with all the bodies
that rise and rise hugging us tightly in their arms
with strongest love.

In the same way that the stones speak, that the earth speaks, I speak to you. And the blindness of my fingers speaks to you as they feel their way over your skull, your nose, your eye sockets, and the infinite sky has collapsed and speaks rising out of the worm-infested sockets of your eyes. And like a landscape of earth rising with the earth our faces start to rise up out of our dead faces and then, as the stones speak, as the earth speaks, I speak to you, corpse of me, love of me, bones of me, small round pupil of all the love that rises and is the song of your eyes looking at me.

I can see you!

And looking at me, blind and looking at me, and blind like the whole sky looking at me, you look down at a country of deserts and you see me. And you see me rising up, and you see me rising and rising and your eyes see my eyes full of earth rising, winged, full of worms but of light in the skies.

And once again I look at you. And surprised like waves in flight our bodies will awaken and as you rise upward you will see below a country of lakes and you will see me. And I will look at you again and you will see me again and your eyes which are lakes bordered by fields of grass will be covered by my eyes and like days dawning the great lakes rising in the dawn will have the color of living flesh. And I will see you again and your flesh will see me again and my living flesh stuck to your living flesh will see you again and the amazed flesh as it hears us will be the color of all the lakes at dawn.

And I will look at you again.

And I will hear you again. Because these words will not die as we ourselves die and the flight of our flesh as it comes alive will stick to us like lakes with the dawn stuck to them and the brief feathers we were will return to the air and the air will be waves of waves and the yous lakes of lakes.

And I will love you again. And from the dead pupils of our eyes the skies will open and the skies as they open will show us the cordilleras down below and you will see a country of volcanoes ascending like a sea to the crater of your eyes. And you will look at me, and you will look at me again, and your eyes looking at me will see the larva of the volcanoes and the volcanoes ascending will touch your pupils and the craters of my pupils will once again touch yours. And the flesh we were will cover us again like the mountains with living larva because a path was made in the solitudes and it was come.

And I will love you again.

And I will love you again and I will tell you come. And you will love me again and you will tell me come. And the sky opening will say to us come because like red larva covering the mountains our flesh will once again cover the snowed bones of all the Andes and I will love you again and it will be come.

And it will be you again. And I just another you of yours. And my eyes as they rise from you will show you down below a country of beaches and the beaches the bones of you which I have been, the teeth of you which I have been, the murdered dead face of you which I have been and which rising up from the empty craters of your eyes showed you the bones of my face changing little by little into yours. And it will be you. And the beaches rising up will be you. And the ocean rising will be you because my love is you and the death of my love is you and the dead beach that begins my life again rising up to the resuscitated beaches of your life is you also.

And it will be you. And far beyond you you will continue being you. And not even you could stop yourself continuing to be you. Not even the beaches where we died or the white-headed waves or death.

And it will be you and again you and the love of our scarred flesh as it rises upward will be embedded in the sky and the sky over the Pacific will be your new face as it joins with the earth. With the earth of you who are and will be forever and ever and the dark beaches and the new epochs of time.

And the sky will stutter in surprise when you come and the words of the sky will sound on my lips like broken gasps. And your lips will seek my lips and seeking them you will see a country of glaciers and icebergs down below and above it the amazed traces of a dead mouth speaking to you. And the sky will fall and my dead mouth will sound with the heavens and then you will hear a horizon of frost and hail and hearing, and then hearing all the blizzards, all the ice-falls, all the glaciers, you will hear my mouth still without flesh and my dead lips as they speak to you will be like two twin blocks of snow.

And my dead mouth will rise out of the snow. And the teeth of your dead mouth will descend through the ice and our reborn lips will be a sky stiffened by cold as they call to each other.

And like a horizon which lives once again in a new horizon our murdered lips will begin again to speak to each other and my mouth will say to you: they killed you and now you are alive. And like the sky, like the snow, like a country of icebergs being born your mouth will say to me: you were dead and today you are alive.

And we will not die. And we will not die again
because like someone who opens herself to a
dream you looked at my remains and saw a
country dismembered in archipelagos and the
remains of our bodies down below were like
archipelagos. And we will not die again and the
channels that open inside the archipelagos will
show you the skies and the skies the sea
corroded by stars and your eyes will never again
be gouged out like dismembered islands falling
onto the waters. Yes, because we will not die
again and these words will live longer than our
solitude, or time, or tempestuous dreams.

Because as long as these words live you will not
die. And if the acid of time and warlike
tempests pull them down, you will not die. And
we will not die again.

And searching for us piece by piece, like a dis-
membered country that comes again into unity,
the sky and the beaches will find each other
again and the beaches the fields and then, like a
new archipelago that rises upward weeping,
our remains will be gathered together and will
not die again. Nor will these channels or islands
or fiords.

And a path will be traced through the solitudes. A new tide will bear us up onto the green earth and leaping with joy the peaks will gaze on the plains and the multitude of our bodies as they rise up will stir the surface of the plains like waves rippling the ocean. Because a path was marked in the solitudes and like a dream that passes through fields of moving grass, the unending fields of our arms greeting the new sky emerged rocking us. The new beach, the new sea opened freeing the imprisoned mountains and it was the earth bringing the dead out of its bowels.

Bringing up our murdered limbs, our legs that moved on their own as if it were the wind that took them and like fields of grass, like waves crossing the sea, we got up out of our corpses crying and it was the sky and the winds and crying.

And we kissed one another's empty pupils and crying. Because a path through the solitudes had been opened and our empty eyes stuck to the sky and I touched the skies of you and you the skies of me in our eyes and then, in the country of volcanoes and deserts, of beaches and icefields, of lakes and oceans, we saw our bodies moving in waves and they were the plains once more.

And they were your plains once more.

Isaiah 11

The INRI of the Landscapes

Epilogue

Hundreds of bodies were thrown over the
mountains, lakes, and sea of Chile. Perhaps a
dream dreamed there were some flowers, there
were some breakers, an ocean, raising them up
out of their tombs in the landscapes. No.

They are dead. The nonexistent flowers were
already said. The nonexistent morning was
already said.

Santiago, Chile
January 2001–March 2002

Translator's Afterword

THIS POEM does not offer redemption; the wound to our common human existence persists, the disappeared dead are still dead. This poem seeks a place where the wound can be included inside the making of a different reality. That place requires a particular type of space, where what has been concealed, expunged from history, can appear. Simply to say "never again," in the face of events such as the mass murders carried out by the Pinochet dictatorship, is not enough. The conditions that allowed such events to take place would have to be changed. Crucially, they pertain to language: the regime's imagination appropriated a whole set of words related to the nation and the land; those who resisted it waged a struggle for the meaning of words, and poetry became a prime part of that struggle. The struggle continued after parliamentary rule was restored. The pathetically inadequate acknowledgment by the elected president, which Raúl Zurita refers to in his introductory statement for *INRI*, was a symptom of that situation.

The struggle for meaning lived on in the language after democracy was restored. The fascist imagination had written its vision of the nation into the Chilean landscape; there was no place in it for the disappeared. But the slain could not be completely obliterated. In *INRI*, the meanings imposed by the dictatorship fall away from the sea, the desert, and the mountains. The physical earth repels the language of the state; instead, it communicates the possibility of an entirely different nation. This is a book that completes itself outside itself, outside literature. In Zurita's words, "In the end what matters is to be capable of constructing a life, not a book."

To be capable of that means engaging with the ways in which reality is currently produced, entering inside them and resisting their logic—in other words, unmaking the laws that determine what can be seen and what cannot be seen. This is where *INRI* places itself. Something not previously seen is made to exist. The unimaginable is imagined. But the unimaginable includes the real; the real that had been denied is acknowledged. This occurs in images before becoming words. The last moments, seen only by the perpetrators, of the disappeared dead, blinded and thrown into the sea and into volcanoes, are permitted to be heard and seen, in a landscape that can receive them; the book says love them. The poetry places before us their living presence, not as specters but as real humans. An event, eliminated from history, is made to occur.

The poetic form of the book, the language in which it invokes new landscapes, is completely interwoven with the ethics it proposes: form and the ethical come together. The land itself speaks, fulfilling the words of Jesus in the gospel: "If they keep silent, the stones will cry out." But "they," in the biblical statement, refers to the disciples; in *INRI*, there is no messiah, no disciples; the earth itself cries out. The voice is irrevocably social.

It's not a matter simply of telling the story of what happened, of finding or inventing a person to speak as witness.

Such a witness would have to speak in a known and familiar language about what the language, the common means of expression, had been made complicit in denying. It is much more than a problem of witnessing.

The resurrection of the disappeared dead is imagined in order that there should be a place for them. The imaginary has first to unbind itself from reality, because reality denies the real. "Poetry comes before religion and philosophy," Zurita has said. The forerunners of *INRI* are Dante's *Divine Comedy* and Rimbaud's *Illuminations*. In both, poetry makes a world that takes the place of the existing order and its language. But it does not do this as simple fantasy. Their poetry unmakes the regime of appearances upon which an existing order of power depends. A good many books of poetry have tried to do exactly that, but nothing of any significance happens unless the force of a book reaches into the deepest levels of how word and image make a world. *INRI* does precisely that. It works by repetition and saturation. We repeatedly pass through the same terrain, but each repetition is a duration, a time that increasingly permits the images to occupy space.

Those strange metaphors with which *INRI* begins not only question received reality but also start to disarrange the order of the senses. If what is really there cannot be seen, it may be necessary to become blind. This is the movement of the book: through hearing, and then touching, the bodies of the disappeared, which had no place, are brought back. To begin again, from a position of blindness: The book in its form insists that mere pity is not enough; something else is needed.

Rather than conventional verses, *INRI* is built out of

sentences. Each one asserts a world, and at the same time negates the existing world. The sentences take up the force of spoken language, but they break the illusion of consensus by speaking out of what is not said. Their strange literalness turns the ordinary against itself, as do the writings of John Bunyan, Abiezer Coppe, and other radical writers of the seventeenth century. The language of *INRI* fuses literal and spiritual space, as also happens in certain seventeenth-century poets, such as George Herbert or Henry Vaughn. Like these poets, Zurita causes speech to turn back through its ordinary meanings towards something strange.

The book imagines the resurrection of the disappeared. Yet Christian redemption is turned into its opposite: "If one died for all, then all died" (2 Corinthians 5:14). There's no notion of redemption through sacrifice, nor any idea of the victim as the person in whom pity can exercise itself as a spurious ethics. What remains of Christian thought is the idea of a common life. We find ourselves, and our capability for love, in the death of the disappeared because they are *our* dead. "Bruno says he has gone back home. Susana also says she has gone back home." The images evoked have no place in the empirical world-as-it-is, but they exist, they make a place. This is the major opening: through repetition, these people become un-disappeared. And since the disappeared could not see because their eyes were gouged out, it's in the senses of hearing and of touch that we may experience the images—hence, in the original edition, the decision to print certain pages in braille. The suggestion is that the events can best be apprehended in the silence of touch before or after words: we have to pass through the ground of meaning as such.

"Strange baits rain from the sky." This is the first movement. The disappeared can be seen and later touched through becoming part of nature. But this is not nature as usually construed, not a subordinate backdrop to human action. Nature itself becomes changed. In a strange but perhaps not so strange coincidence, *INRI* begins with virtually the same metaphor as the well-known 1937 poem and subsequent song "Strange Fruit," which was recorded by Billie Holiday and which protests the murder by lynching of black Americans. But instead of seeing nature as stained by murder, *INRI* demands that nature itself be prized away from language as it is, just as Holiday's voice prizes the words of "Strange Fruit" away from ordinary meaning. The mountains, sea, and desert have the force of a landscape first seen, of a language not previously heard; something occurs that bypasses the selective filters of normalization, filters that protect reality from its overthrow. The images of Chile seen in *INRI* do not result from individual feeling projected onto nature: they do not allow that type of individualism. They call on our capacity for justice, for a common life inside the deepest empathy.

—*William Rowe*